Buddy Systems, Inc., Petitioner, v. Exer Genie, Inc., and E. E. Holkesvick. U.S. Supreme Court Transcript of Record with Supporting Pleadings

Table of Contents

Buddy Systems, Inc., Petitioner, v. Exer Genie, Inc., and E. E. Holkesvick. U.S. Supreme Court Transcript of Record with Supporting Pleadings

V J MCALPIN, CHARLES E WILLS

Buddy Systems, Inc., Petitioner, v. Exer Genie, Inc., and E. E. Holkesvick.
Petition / V J MCALPIN / 1976 / 76-1056 / 431 U.S. 903 / 97 S.Ct. 1694 / 52 L.Ed.2d 387 / 2-1-1977
Buddy Systems, Inc., Petitioner, v. Exer Genie, Inc., and E. E. Holkesvick.
Brief in Opposition (P) / CHARLES E WILLS / 1976 / 76-1056 / 431 U.S. 903 / 97 S.Ct. 1694 / 52 L.Ed.2d 387 / 4-11-1977

76-1056

In the Supreme Court of the United States

OCTOBER TERM, 1976

No._____

76-1056 972

BUDDY SYSTEMS, INC., a corporation,

Petitioner,

vs.

EXER-GENIE, INC., a corporation, and
E. E. HOLKESVICK,

Respondents.

PETITION FOR WRIT OF CERTIORARI
FROM THE UNITED STATES COURT OF APPEALS
FOR THE NINTH CIRCUIT

V. J. McALPIN
McALPIN, DOONAN & SEESE
211 South Citrus
Covina, California 91723
(213) 331-6376

Attorney for Petitioner

i

TOPICAL INDEX

APPENDIX

TABLE OF AUTHORITIES CITED

Cases

Statutes

Rules

iv

Law Reviews

In the Supreme Court of the United States

OCTOBER TERM, 1976

No. _____

BUDDY SYSTEMS, INC., a corporation,

Petitioner,

vs.

EXER-GENIE, INC., a corporation, and E. E. Holkesvick,

Respondents.

PETITION FOR WRIT OF CERTIORARI
FROM THE UNITED STATES COURT OF APPEALS
FOR THE NINTH CIRCUIT

To the Honorable Chief Justice and Associate Justices of the Supreme Court of the United States:

Petitioner respectfully prays that a Writ of Certiorari issue to review the judgment and opinion of the United States Court of Appeals for the Ninth Circuit in the above-entitled cause.

I.

OPINIONS BELOW

The opinion of the Court of Appeals is reproduced in the Appendix at p. 1-14. The order of the Court of Appeals denying Rehearing is set forth in the Appendix at p. 15.[1]

---

[1] References to the Appendix annexed hereto are designated as "APP." followed by the page number. All emphases are Petitioner's, unless otherwise stated.

II.

JURISDICTION

The opinion of the Court of Appeals was entered on September 27, 1976.

Petitioner's Petition for Rehearing *en banc* was denied on November 4, 1976.

This Court has jurisdiction to review the Opinion of the Court of Appeals pursuant to 28 U.S.C. 1254(1).

III.

QUESTIONS PRESENTED FOR REVIEW

1.   Whether the opinion of the Court of Appeals in the instant matter presents a conflict among the Circuits regarding the issue of jurisdiction in similar matters.

2.   Whether the Court of Appeals can act to defeat the purpose of Rule 65(c) of the Federal Rules of Civil Procedure thereby foreclosing Petitioner's claim for damages suffered as a result of a wrongful injunction?

3.   Should an error of the United States District Court Clerk be considered in determining the propriety of the granting of this Petition for a Writ of Certiorari?

IV.

STATUTES AND RULES INVOLVED

This Cause involves 28 U.S.C. 1352 (APP.16), Rule 65(c) of the Federal Rules of Civil Procedure (APP.16), and Rule 65.1 of the Federal Rules of Civil Procedure (APP.16).

V.

CONCISE STATEMENT OF THE CASE

In 1968, Respondents *Exer-Genie* and *E.E. Holkesvick* brought an action against Petitioner Buddy Systems and several other defendants for infringement of a patent used in the manufacture of an exercise device. Exer-Genie sought and secured a preliminary injunction in order to restrain Buddy

Systems from making or selling a competitive exercise device. The preliminary injunction was granted on the conditions that Exer-Genie post security in the amount of $100,000.00 "by a corporate surety bond, or a treasury bond or a certificate of deposit payable to Clerk, United States District Court, for the payment of such costs and damages as may be incurred or suffered by any party who is found to be wrongfully enjoined or restrained." Exer-Genie filed a certificate of deposit and the District Court issued a writ of injunction. No Appeal was taken by Buddy Systems from the issuance of the preliminary injunction.

After a trial on the merits, the district judge found the patent was valid and infringed and made the preliminary injunction permanent, but lesser in scope than the preliminary injunction. He concluded the preliminary injunction was lawfully and regularly issued and therefore Exer-Genie was entitled to have the security exonerated.

Buddy Systems objected to the exoneration of the security prior to the expiration of the time to appeal. The district judge afforded Buddy Systems an opportunity to submit in writing any argument it might have in support of its objection, and Buddy Systems did submit such argument to the district judge in its Objections to the Findings of Fact and Conclusions of Law and Judgment as proposed by Plaintiffs, but the judgment was entered on August 15, 1969 and ordered the bond exonerated. The bond was actually released by the district court clerk on August 18, 1969, but such fact was not noted on the official docket sheet of the District Court Clerk at that time.

On Appeal, the district court's judgment was reversed and the Court of Appeals held the Exer-Genie was invalid as to the claims involved. *Exer-Genie, Inc. v. McDonald, et al.*, 453 F. 2d 132 (Ninth Cir. 1971), *cert. denied*, 405 U.S. 1075 (1972). Buddy Systems did not challenge the exoneration of the bond as premature and erroneous, and the Ninth Circuit did not reach that issue on appeal.

After said decision of the Ninth Circuit was entered on September 14, 1971, Buddy Systems first discovered that the bond was actually released on August 18, 1969. Whereupon, a motion was made by Buddy Systems on December 6, 1971, to compel plaintiffs Exer-Genie and Holkesvick to redeposit the security given for the preliminary injunction. The district court denied said motion.

However, the court stated: "The Court is of the view that the issue is still open and may and should be asserted by the defendant . . . "

After the denial of certiorari of this Court, Buddy Systems commenced the present suit to recover damages for the wrongful issuance of the preliminary injunction, invoking 28 U.S.C. 1352 as the sole jurisdictional basis for its suit.

Buddy Systems again moved the district court in the present suit to compel Exer-Genie to redeposit the security which had been released earlier. The motion was denied without prejudice, and the trial proceeded without the bond actually being redeposited. A judgment was entered awarding damages to Buddy Systems in the sum of $35,000.00.

Several issues were raised on appeal of the present action by Exer-Genie, but the Court of Appeals considered only one: Whether the district court had subject matter jurisdiction over the suit pursuant to section 1352?

Following the submission of appeal briefs, oral argument was heard on October 8, 1975, at which time Circuit Judge Ely admonished counsel for both parties to limit their argument to the question of damages only, and commented to counsel for Exer-Genie that "You cannot frustrate jurisdiction by withdrawing the security."

However, the opinion on appeal concluded that since the bond had been exonerated, there was no bond upon which an action could be brought, and thus the district court did not have jurisdiction of the subject matter.

VI.

ARGUMENT

1. Certiorari Should Be Granted To Resolve A Conflict Which Exists Between Two Courts Of Appeals On An Issue Of Importance.

There is no question that Certiorari is discretionary, but when a conflict exists among the Circuits, the Supreme Court has consistently granted Certiorari to resolve such conflicts.

The decision of the Ninth Circuit below is in direct conflict with the case of *Atomic Oil Co. v. Bardahl Oil Co.*, (10th Circuit 1969) 419 F. 2d 1097, *cert. denied*, 397 U.S. 1063 (1970), wherein a preliminary injunction was granted by the district court. The injunction was made permanent, but lesser in scope than the preliminary injunction. After a trial on the merits, the bond for the original preliminary injunction was in the sum of $50,000.00, which was posted by Atomic Oil by the assignment of a $50,000.00 savings account. A new bond in the sum of $25,000.00 was posted upon the issuance of the permanent injunction, and the original $50,000.00 bond was ordered released and dissolved the preliminary injunction.

The district court judgment for plaintiff was reversed by the 10th Circuit. Whereupon, Bardahl sought recovery in an independent action on both bonds for the "costs and damages," which it incurred as a result of the erroneous issuance of the injunctions. The damages suffered by Bardahl were allegedly substantially greater than the aggregate amount of the injunctive bonds. Judgment for Bardahl was granted in the District Court and affirmed in the Appellate Court and recovery was permitted on both bonds.

The Court below summarily stated that it disagreed with the holding of the *Atomic Oil Co. v. Bardahl Oil Co., supra*, 419 F. 2d 1097.

The facts in the present case are similar to those in the *Atomic Oil Co. v. Bardahl Oil Co.* case, *supra*. The respondent. Exer-Genie, sought and secured a preliminary injunction. Exer-Genie posted its own $100,000.00 certificate of deposit. After a trial on the merits, the issuing court exonerated the security for the bond, and issued a permanent injunction. The permanent injunction was lesser in scope than the preliminary injunction in that it was limited to the accused device, whereas the preliminary injunction could be read directly on the prior art.

Upon appeal, the district court's judgment was reversed and Buddy Systems brought an independent action on the bond for the preliminary injunction for its costs and damages suffered as a result of the preliminary injunction. The judgment was in the amount of $35,000.00 in favor of Buddy Systems, and Exer-Genie appealed arguing, among other things, the lack of jurisdiction of the district court over the subject matter of the action.

There is no question that the bond was originally posted pursuant to the *Rule 65 (c)* of the *Federal Rules of Civil Procedure.* Likewise, there is no question that *Section 1352* of Title 28, U.S.C. grants jurisdiction to the district courts to hear an action on a bond executed pursuant to Rule 65 (c).

The Ninth Circuit concluded that the district court employed a *fiction* to overcome the fact that the bond was no longer posted with the clerk. The district court had stated that the bond has two separate aspects: (1) a promise to make the defendant whole in case the preliminary injunction is improperly granted and damages result, and (2) the deposit of security from which payment for any damages will be obtained, and that the promise continues to be enforceable even after the security is exonerated.

The Ninth Circuit reasoned "that even if a duty independent of the security posted under Rule 65 can be implied, the district court's theory that a suit to enforce that duty is an action 'on a bond' finds no justification in *common law bond history.*" (Emphasis added.)

However, this matter is not involved with common law bond history, but rather with the present day statutory law and its requirements as set forth in Rule 65 (c). The duty to make whole the injured party, who has been wrongfully enjoined, is the paramount reason for the enactment of said rule.

In *Atomic Oil Co. v. Bardahl Oil Co., supra*, 419 F. 2d at 1100-1101, the court there stated, "Rule 65 (c) states in *mandatory* language that the giving of security is an *absolute condition* precedent to the issuance of a preliminary injunction. It imparts no discretion to the trial court to mitigate or nullify that undertaking after the injunction has issued." (Emphasis added.)

" . . . It is the duty of a court of equity granting injunctive relief to do so upon conditions that will protect all * * * whose interests the injunction may affect." *Inland Steel Co. v. U.S.*, 306 U.S. 153, 59 S.Ct. 415, 417, 83 L.Ed. 557."

The language of the court of appeals for the Ninth Circuit is contrary to the above-quoted citations and states in the opinion: "But more importantly, no underlying duty to recompense the victim of wrongful provisional relief independent of the security instrument may be implied. It is a well-settled rule that there can be no recovery for damages sustained by a wrongful issuance of a preliminary injunction in the absence of a bond. [Citations] ."

The Court of Appeals relies on the cases of *United Bonding Insurance Co. v. Alexander*, 413 F. 2d 1025, 1026 (5th Cir. 1969), which was a subrogation suit by a bonding company against 21 postal employees for various losses attributed to the employees' failure to perform their duties faithfully. The district court dismissed the action for lack of requisite jurisdictional amount, because no single claim exceeded $2500.00. The bonding company claimed that Title 28 U.S.C. § 1352 conferred jurisdiction regardless of the amount in controversy. The Court of Appeals affirmed the district court and held "Section 1352 is applicable only to a suit *on a bond*, which means a suit against one bound by its terms for a breach of duty arising under it. *The two-party agreement* between the Post Office Department and the United Bonding cannot be stretched to permit suit against *postal employees, who were not parties to it.*" (Emphasis added.)

It would seem as though the Ninth Circuit was stretching to attempt to utilize the language of *United Bonding* to fit the present action. The promise to pay existed only between United Bonding and the Post Office Department. There was no promise by the postal employees to repay the bonding company for its loss.

However, in the instant case the promise to pay for damages suffered by the wrongful injunction did exist between the parties to this suit, and thus this action does fall under Section 1352.

Further reliance by the Ninth Circuit in this case on the 1881 case of *Russell v. Farley*, 105 U.S. 433, 437 (1881), which holds that when the *security posted to satisfy a bond* is no longer equitably required, the court which ordered the bond must have the power to release it and, having so done, no appellate jurisdiction exists to assess damages resulting from the litigation after the trial court refuses to do so.

The *Russell v. Farley* case was decided *prior* to the enactment of Rule 65 (c) and 65.1. It is, however, interesting to note that the wording "*security posted to satisfy a bond,*" tends to uphold the reasoning of the district court in the instant matter, *i.e.*, the bond is the promise, and the security is the amount deposited from which payment for damages may be obtained.

The *Atomic Oil Co. v. Bardahl Oil Co.* case, *supra*, further stated, "Moreover, since the holding of *Russell v. Farley* was expressly predicated upon the absence of an applicable court rule on statute, the presence of Rule 65 (c) would seem to cast great doubt upon the continued viability of the *Russell v. Farley* rule in cases arising under the Federal Rules of Civil Procedure."

Even the Ninth Circuit in the case of *Golden Gate Mechanical Contractors Association v. Seaboard Surety Co.*, 389 F. 2d 892 (9th Cir. 1968), has recognized that exonerating a bond does not wipe out liability of a surety. Although this was a diversity jurisdiction case, it held: "There is no merit to Seaboard's contention that the exoneration of the bonds operated to wipe out liability. The exoneration would operate only prospectively."

Further, as stated in *Northeast Airlines v. Nationwide Charters and Conventions, Inc.*, 413 F. 2d 335 (1st Cir. 1969) at p. 338, "We think the District Court erred, however, in ordering the plaintiff's security deposit be released and refunded. The purpose of the security required by Rule 65 (c) Fed. R. Civ. P. to be furnished to obtain a preliminary injunction is in the words of the Rule 'for the payment of such costs and damages as may be incurred or suffered by any party who is found to have been wrongfully enjoined or restrained.' . . . We think the defendants are entitled to an opportunity to proceed against Northeast or its security for whatever damages, if any, they may be able to establish that they suffered by reason of the overbreadth of the preliminary injunction."

The trial court in the present action concurred with the reasoning of the *Northeast Airlines* and *Atomic Oil* cases in permitting Plaintiff Buddy Systems to seek damages for the wrongful injunction.

Therefore, based upon the conflicting decisions between the Ninth Circuit and the cases cited from the First and Tenth Circuits, it is necessary for this Court to state whether a district court may have jurisdiction on a bond issued pursuant to Rule 65 (c), but which has been exonerated prior to a final determination of the case for which it was issued.

2. May The Court Of Appeals Act To Defeat The Purpose Of Rule 65(c) Of The Federal Rules of Civil Procedure, Thereby Foreclosing Petitioner's Claim For Damages Suffered As A Result Of A Wrongful Injunction?

The manifest purpose of Rule 65 (c) is its mandatory requirement of the posting of security prior to the issuance of a restraining order or preliminary injunction, and which is "for the payment of such costs and damages as may be incurred or suffered by any party who is found to have been wrongfully enjoined or restrained."

Rule 65.1 states "each surety upon a bond or undertaking under this rule submits himself to the *jurisdiction* of the court and *irrevocably* appoints the clerk of the court as his agent upon whom any papers affecting his liability on the bond or undertaking may be served." (Emphasis added.)

The amount of the security is to be determined by the issuing court in the exercise of its sound discretion, and limits the amount of damages recoverable under the bond should it later be determined that the issuance of the injunction was improvidently granted.

The enactment of Rule 65 (c) was done for the express purpose of protecting the interests of those who were subsequently found to have been wrongfully enjoined. It is merely an extension of and guidelines for the enforcement of the old maxim: "He who seeks equity must do equity."

In the instant case, Exer-Genie sought the special power of the original court in securing the preliminary injunction. Exer-Genie complied with Rule 65 (c) and the order of the injunction court[2] by posting the security in the form of a

---

[2] The district court's order required that:

"Pursuant to Rule 65 (c) of the Federal Rules of Civil Procedure, the plaintiffs herein shall give security in the sum of One Hundred Thousand Dollars ($100,000.00), by a corporate surety bond, or by a treasury bond or a certificate

certificate of deposit as required by the court order.

The original judgment which held the patent claims of Exer-Genie valid was later reversed, *Exer-Genie, Inc. v. McDonald, et al.*, 453 F. 2d 132 (9th Cir. 1971) *cert. denied*, 405 U.S. 1075 (1972). However, the original trial court nor the appellate court did not attempt to assess any damages for the issuance of the injunction.

On appeal of the instant case, the appeals court placed great reliance on the case of *Russell v. Farley*, 105 U.S. 433, 437 (1881) cited by Exer-Genie as dispositive of the issue of jurisdiction.

However, the holding of *Russell v. Farley* was expressly predicated upon the absence of an applicable court rule or statute, and the Supreme Court in its opinion stated:

> " * * * [N]o Act of Congress, or rule of this Court, has ever been passed or adopted on this subject. The Courts of the United States, therefore, must still be governed in the matter by the general principles and usages of equity." 105 U.S. at 441.

The district court in this matter obviously found that (1) The bond and security was posted in the original action pursuant to the court order and Rule 65 (c), and (2) determined there was jurisdiction under Section 1352 based on the express wording of the original court order and Rule 65 (c).

Again, the language of Rule 65.1 itself makes it imperative that a surety upon a bond or undertaking submit himself to the *jurisdiction* of the court and *irrevocably* appoints the clerk of the court as his agent upon whom any papers affecting his liability on the bond or undertaking may be served.

---

of deposit payable to the Clerk, United States District Court, for the payment of such costs and damages as may be incurred or suffered by any party who is found to be wrongfully enjoined or restrained."

Even in the absence of Rule 65 (c), *Russell v. Farley* cannot be successfully applied to eliminate jurisdiction in this case, because the court that issued the injunction in the first proceeding only released or exonerated the security at the point in time. This is substantiated by the statement of the same court at the time of Buddy Systems' motion to compel the redeposit of the security on December 6, 1971, when the injunctive court stated: "I did not adjudicate at any prior time, and had no intention of adjudicating, whether defendants suffered any damage from the preliminary injunction, if the same was properly granted. The court is of the view that the issue is still open and may and should be asserted by the defendant . . ."

"MR. WILLS: Is that 'May'?"

"THE COURT: May and should be asserted by defendant, if defendant eventually prevails on the main action, in a separate, separate independent action."

Reporter's Transcript of Hearing
on December 6, 1971.

Thus, the order of the injunctive court was plainly not a negation of damages under the bond.

At the time of the hearing on said motion on December 6, 1971, the prior case was before the United States Courts of Appeals for the Ninth Circuit, pending the filing of a petition for Certiorari to the Supreme Court, which was ultimately denied as aforesaid.

Upon the denial of Exer-Genie's petition for Certiorari by the Supreme Court, there was a final determination that the preliminary injunction was wrongful because the patent in question had been held to be invalid as to the claims involved.

Although there was no specific determination in the prior matter by the Appeals Court that the injunction was wrongful, it is a *matter of law* that an injunction granted on the assumption of an alleged valid patent is wrongful *ab initio* when it is ultimately determined that the patent is invalid. In a patent case, the validity of the patent is a prerequisite to the issuance of a preliminary injunction. *Pacific Cage & Screen Co. v. Continental Cage Corp.*, 259 F. 2d 87 (9th Cir. 1958).

Thus, when the Ninth Circuit reversed the decision of the district court in *Exer-Genie v. McDonald*, 453 F. 2d 132 (1971), and Certiorari was denied, 405 U.S. 1075 (1972), a "final determination" was established under which the party who was wrongfully enjoined could then proceed to enforce the liability of the surety under Rule 65.1 of the Federal Rules of Civil Procedure.

It is a basic rule of law that there is no final determination until all appeals have been exhausted. In the language of the Supreme Court, a final decision must generally be "one which ends the litigation . . . and leaves nothing for the Court to do but execute the judgment."

Catlin v. United States, (1945)
324 U.S. 229, 65 S.Ct. 631,
89 L.Ed. 911.

It would have been premature for Buddy Systems to have brought an action on the bond prior to the denial of Exer-Genie's petition for Certiorari. However, the Court of Appeals below states that Buddy Systems' failure to raise the wrongful exoneration order on appeal was a blunder, which results in the loss of purpose of Rule 65 (c).

The Ninth Circuit states: "We are here dealing with the *exceptional* case where a party has been wrongfully enjoined, the district court erroneously has exonerated the bond and the party, without excuse, has failed to appeal this error." (Emphasis added.)

The Ninth Circuit obviously recognized that (1) the injunction was wrongful, and (2) that the exoneration of the bond was in error, but fails to apply the imperative conditions set forth in Rule 65 (c) against Respondent Exer-Genie.

Further, the Appeals Court refused to apply principles of equity set forth in *Russell v. Farley*, 105 U.S. at 441, by its dicta in stating: "If we adopted its approach, sureties would be uncertain as to the termination of their liability and bonding costs could increase to reflect this uncertainty. *Cf. Northern Trust Co. v. Edenborn*, 39 F. Supp. 607 (W.D. LA. 1941). An increase in bonding costs would have a deterrent effect on the meritorious claims of indigents who seek provisional injunctive relief under Rule 65. See Dobbs, *Provisional Injunctive Relief*, 52 N. Car. L. Rev. at 1112-17; Blood, *Injunction Bonds: Equal Protection for the Indigent*, 11 S.Tex. L.J. 16 (1969). District Courts may well react to higher bond costs by exercising discretion to require bonds of lower amounts. Thus, the net result of adopting a pro-recovery approach here could well be to subject more defendants to the prospect of inadequate relief for wrongfully issued injunctions."

The above-quoted statement is wrought with suppositions concerning the increase in bonding costs to indigents who seek provisional injunctive relief, and alludes to equitable principles without granting equity itself or applying the provisions of Rule 65 (c).

The purpose of Rule 65 (c) is not to protect the interests of sureties, but rather is to protect the interests of persons who have been wrongfully enjoined.

The requirement of security under Rule 65 (c) is rooted in the belief that a defendant deserves protection against an improvidently issued injunction. That protection consists of a promise that the defendant will be reimbursed for losses suffered if it turns out that the injunction was issued in error.

3.   Should An Error Of The United States District Court Clerk Be Considered To Determine Whether This Petition Should be Granted?

The Court of Appeals below opines that the failure of Buddy Systems to raise the issue of the exoneration of the bond on appeal in the first case is fatal, and refused to consider the facts that were presented by Buddy Systems in its Petition for Rehearing concerning the reason Buddy Systems did not raise the erroneous order of exoneration of the bond on appeal.

It is a policy of this court and other appellate courts that a question presented will be deemed to include every subsidiary question fairly comprised therein, and it has been held that irrelevant matters should be excluded.

The principal question to be determined at the time of the filing of the original appeal was the validity of the patent in question. All other issues were secondary and in some degree, contingent upon the validity issue.

At the time of the filing of the Notice of Appeal, in the case of *Exer-Genie v. McDonald*, 453 F. 2d 132 (9th Cir. 1970), the official docket sheet of the United States District Court Clerk indicated that the bond for the preliminary injunction was still posted, or at least did not reveal that it had been released. (Clerk's Record Transmitted on Appeal of Case No. 68-751-IH, pages 290-295.)

Counsel for Buddy Systems did not argue the exoneration of the bond on appeal, because according to the official court record the bond was still on deposit, and such an argument would have been unnecessarily encumbering the record with irrelevant or moot questions.

When the U.S. District Court Clerk transmitted the Official Record on Appeal to the Ninth Circuit on April 27, 1970, said records still did not reflect the fact that the security for the bond had been released to counsel for Exer-Genie on August 18, 1969.

Subsequent to the decision of the Ninth Circuit in *Exer-Genie v. McDonald*, 453 F. 2d 132, wherein the decision of the district court was reversed, it was *first* discovered that the security for the bond given by Exer-Genie for the preliminary injunction had, in fact, been released on August 18, 1969, only three days after the entry of the judgment, which was prior to the expiration of the time to appeal.

The entry noting the fact of the release of the security has now been inserted at the bottom of page 5 in handwriting. This handwritten notation was not present at the time the record was transmitted by the clerk on appeal. Surely, an appellant should be able to rely on the official record of the U.S. District Court Clerk in matters of such importance. This error was most definietly not the fault of Petitioner, and should be considered in granting this petition.

CONCLUSION

Therefore, Petitioner contends (1) the Court of Appeals erred in ruling that the district court did not have jurisdiction on the bond in question; (2) it has been established by the judgment that Petitioner has suffered substantial harm as a result of the preliminary injunction; (3) Petitioner should not be held guilty of failing to appeal the order of exoneration of the bond, when the security was apparently still posted according to the official court docket sheet; and (4) Petitioner has no other remedy at law, and if this petition for a Writ of Certiorari is not granted, Petitioner will be completely foreclosed of its rights given under Rule 65 (c).

Because of the foregoing reasons, it is respectfully requested that this Court grant the petition and issue a Writ of Certiorari to review the opinion and judgment of the Court of Appeals.

Respectfully submitted,

V.J. McAlpin,
Counsel for Petitioner

APPENDIX

UNITED STATES COURT OF APPEALS

FOR THE NINTH CIRCUIT

BUDDY SYSTEMS, INC.
a California Corporation,
Plaintiff-Appellee,

vs.

No. 74-1639

EXER-GENIE, INC., a Corporation,
and E. E. HOLKESVICK,
Defendants-Appellants

OPINION

(September 27, 1976)

Appeal from the United States District Court

for the Central District of California

Before: ELY and WALLACE, Circuit Judges,

and RENFREW,* District Judge

WALLACE, Circuit Judge:

Exer-Genie, Inc., and Holkesvick (Exer-Genie) appeal
from a judgment awarding damages to Buddy Systems, Inc.
for the wrongful issuance of a preliminary injunction obtained by Exer-Genie in a prior action. The issue we must
decide is whether a district court may entertain jurisdiction pursuant to 28 U.S.C. §1352[1] over a suit on an injunction bond after the bond has been exonerated. We hold

---

*Honorable Charles B. Renfrew, United States District Judge,
Northern District of California, sitting by designation.
   [1]The district courts shall have original jurisdiction, concurrent with State courts, of any action on
   a bond executed under any law of the United States.
28 U.S.C. §1352

-1-

that the district court was without jurisdiction to hear this suit and therefore reverse.

1

In 1968 Exer-Genie brought suit against Buddy Systems and several other defendants for infringement of a patent used in the manufacture of an exercise device. Exer-Genie moved for a preliminary injunction in order to restrain Buddy Systems from making or selling a competitive exercise device. The preliminary injunction was granted on the condition that Exer-Genie post security in the amount of $100,000.[2] Exer-Genie filed a certificate of deposit and the district court issued a writ of injuntion. Buddy Systems did not appeal from the issuance of the preliminary injunction.

After a trial on the merits, the district judge found that Exer-Genie's patent was valid and had been infringed and therefore made the preliminary injunction permanent. He concluded that

"(t)he preliminary injunction was lawfully and regularly issued by the Court and therefore the plaintiffs (pursuant to their request) are entitled to have exonerated the security which they posted."

[2]The district court's order required that:
Pursuant to Rule 65(c) of the Federal Rules of Civil Procedure, the plaintiffs herein shall give security in the sum of One Hundred Thousand Dollars ($100,000.00), by a corporate surety bond, or by a treasury bond or a certificate of deposit payable to Clerk, United States District Court, for the payment of such costs and damages as may be incurred or suffered by any party who is found to be wrongfully enjoined or restrained.

Buddy Systems objected to the exoneration of the security before the time for appeal had expired. The district judge afforded Buddy Systems an opportunity to submit in writing any authority it might have in support of its objection, but Buddy Systems failed to do so. The final judgment ordered the injunction bond exonerated.

On appeal, we reversed the district court's judgment and held that Exer-Genie's patents were invalid. Exer-Genie, Inc. v. McDonald, 453 F.2d 132 (9th Cir. 1971), cert. denied, 405 U.S. 1075 (1972). Buddy Systems did not challenge the exoneration of the bond as premature and erroneous and we did not reach that issue on appeal.

After our decision, Buddy Systems filed the present suit to recover damages for the wrongful issuance of a preliminary injunction, invoking 28 U.S.C. §1352 as the sole jurisdictional basis for its suit. It then moved to compel Exer-Genie to redeposit the security which had been released earlier. The motion was denied and the trial proceeded with no bond in existence. A judgment was entered awarding $35,000 damages to Buddy Systems.

Exer-Genie raises several issues in its appeal from this second judgment. We need consider only one: whether the district court had subject matter jurisdiction over the suit pursuant to section 1352. Since we answer this question in the negative, we need not reach the remaining issues.

Section 1352 grants jurisdiction to hear an "action on a bond" executed pursuant to Rule 65(c), Fed. R. Civ. P.

(security required for issuance of preliminary injunction).
In this case, the simple fact is that the bond had been exonerated; therefore, there was no bond upon which an action
could be brought. To overcome what appears to be obvious,
the district court employed a fiction. It concluded that a
bond and the security are distinguishable and that here the
bond continued in existence after the security was discharged
upon exoneration. Buddy Systems adds a different theory on
appeal. It concludes that once a bond is executed, any district court may later entertain jurisdiction over an action
for wrongful issuance of an injunction, regardless whether
the bond has been exonerated. Neither theory supports
jurisdiction.

II

The district court reasoned that a bond has two separate aspects: it involves (1) a promise to make the defendant whole in case the preliminary injunction is improperly granted and damages result and (2) the deposit of security from which payment for any damages will be obtained.
The promise continues to be enforceable even after the
security is exonerated, the court argued, and a suit on the
promise is a suit "on a bond" within the meaning of section
1352. This theory has a superficial plausibility, but it
finds little support in history or authority.

While we hesitate to resurrect ancient law, common
law history is instructive. The practice of giving tangible

items as security, called "gage," in order to acquire
credit arose before any consensual theory of contract obli-
gation emerged. The creditor took possession of the gage
and retained it until he was repaid. But there was no
underlying duty on the part of the debtor--if he failed to
pay, the creditor held the security, but had no action on
the debt. A surety was referred to as a "pledge," and was
at first literally "an animated gage. . . delivered over
to slavery but subject to redemption." 2 F. Pollock &
F. Maitland, The History of English Law 185-86 (2d ed.
1899).

Although these devices were used for a number of purposes, they also served a role very similar to that of the
Rule 65 injunction bond involved in this case. For example,
at early common law the plaintiff in a replevin action
against a distrainor was required to give "gage and pledge"
--i.e., a surety's bond. Id. at 577; see Dobbs, Should
Security be Required as a Pre-Condition to Provisional Injunction relief? 52 N. Car. L. Rev. 1091, 1093 (1974).

At later common law, a bond was a sealed and delivered
instrument binding the obligor to pay a sum of money.
1A A. Corbin, Contracts, §258, at 455 (1963). It did not
need to be supported by consideration. 12 Halsbury's Laws
of England §1400 (4th ed. 1975). While common law bonds
may be used for many purposes, including security for the
performance of independent obligations, see id. §1387, the
term "bond does not refer to the duty whose performance is
secured, but only to the security itself. See id. 1385.[3]

Thus even if a duty independent of the security posted under Rule 65 can be implied, the district court's theory that a suit to enforce that duty is an action "on a bond" finds no justification in common law bond history. This was the construction given to section 1352 in United Bonding Insurance Co. v. Alexander, 413 F.2d 1025, 1026 (5th Cir. 1969), where the court held that an action by the obligor on a duty implied by the bond was not a suit "on a bond" within the meaning of section 1352 over a suit on any alleged promise independent of the security instrument.

But more importantly, no underlying duty to recompense the victim of wrongful provisional relief independent of the security instrument may be implied. It is a well-settled rule that there can be no recovery for damages sustained by a wrongful issuance of a preliminary injunction in the absence of a bond, Russell v. Farley, 105 U.S. 433, 437 (1881); Benz v. Compania Naviera Hidalgo, S.A. 205 F.2d 944, 947-48 (9th Cir.) (on petition for rehearing), cert. denied, 346 U.S. 885 (1953), unless the defendant sues for malicious prosecution or on a theory of unjust enrichment, Northern Oil Co. v. Socony Mobil Oil Co., 347 F.2d 81, 83 (2d Cir. 1965); 11 C. Wright & A. Miller, Federal Practice and Procedure §2973 at 652 (1973); see 7 U. Chi. L. Rev. 382 (1940). If a bond is posted, liability is limited by the

---

[3]There is one exception. Where a bond (specialty) is co-extensive with a simple contract debt secured by it, the contract debt is deemed to have merged into the specialty. 12 Halsbury's Laws of England §1411 (4th ed. 1975).

terms of the bond or the order of the court that required
the posting. See 11 Wright & Miller, supra, §2973, at 652;
Comment, The Triggering of Liability on Injunction Bonds,
52 N. Car. L. Rev. 1252, 1258 (1974).[4] The district court's
theory that a duty in addition to those created by the
court's order may be implied is directly opposed to these
settled rules.[5]

Futhermore, we do not find any special circumstances
in this case to justify a departure from these settled
rules. The district judge conditioned the preliminary
injunction "(u) pon the giving of security" in the form of
"a corporate surety bond, or by a treasury bond or a certificate of deposit payable to Clerk." Exer-Genie submitted
a certificate of deposit. There was nothing said about any
independent promise. After trial, the district court ordered that the security be returned to Exer-Genie without
any qualification or condition at all. The court specifically rejected Buddy Systems' plea that the security be
retained pending appeal. This order completely discharged
the relationship the district court had previously

---

[4]For example, liability on the bond is not diminished when
parties consent to a modification of a preliminary injunction which has the effect of reducing the potential liability on the bond, even where the surety has not been noti-
fied of the agreement. Future Fashions, Inc. v. American
Surety Co., 58 F. Supp. 36, 37-38 (S.D.N.Y. 1944).

[5]A few states do allow recovery for the erroneous but non-
malicious issue of an injunction in the absence of a bond
or in excess of its limits. See Note, Interlocutory Injunctions and the Injunction Bond, 73 Harv. L. Rev. 333,
344-46 (1959).

24

established; there was nothing left upon which Buddy
Systems could bring this action. See 11 Wright & Miller,
supra, §2973, at 652-53.

Neither do we find any support for the district court's
theory in the language of Rules 65(c)[6] and 65.1.[7] The rules
simply refer to "the giving of security" "in the form of
a bond or stipulation or other undertaking." The statutory predecessors of Rule 65(c) likewise refer soley to a
security device.[8] Thus we conclude that implied promise

---

[6]Rule 65(c) provides in part:
   No restraining order or preliminary injunction shall
   issue except upon the giving of security by the applicant, in such sum as the court deems proper, for the
   payment of such costs and damages as may be incurred
   or suffered by any party who is found to have been
   wrongfully enjoined or restrained. . . .
      The provisions of Rule 65.1 apply to a surety upon
   a bond or undertaking under this rule.
Fed. R. Civ. P. 65(c).
[7]Rule 65.1 provides in part:
   Whenever . . . security is given in the form of a
   bond or stipulation or other undertaking with one or
   more sureties, each surety('s) . . . liability on the
   bond or undertaking . . . may be enforced on motion
   without the necessity of an independent action.
Fed. R. Civ. P. 65.1.
[8]Rule 65(c) borrows substantially the same language used
in Section 382 of the Judicial Code of 1926, 44 Stat., pt.
1, 909, which in turn employed the language of section 18
of the Clayton Act, ch. 323, 38 Stat. 738 (1914):
   (N)o restraining order or interlocutory order of
   injunction shall issue, except upon the giving of
   security by the applicant in such sum as the court
   or judge may deem proper, conditioned upon the payment of such costs and damages as may be incurred or
   suffered by any party who may be found to have been
   wrongfully enjoined or restrained thereby.
Section 17 of the Clayton Act, ch. 323, 38 Stat. 737 (1914)
had repealed section 263 of the Judiciary Act of 1911, ch.
231, 36 Stat. 1162, which had provided that a preliminary
injunction "may be granted with or without security, in
the discretion of the court or judge." A predecessor
statute had used nearly identical language, Act of June 1,
1872, ch. 255, §7, 17 Stat. 197.

upon which the district court based liability is not a
"bond" within the meaning of section 1352 and more importantly that no such promise is implied by a Rule 65 order
to post security. Once the security is returned to the
plaintiff there can no longer be a section 1352 action "on
a bond." To the extent that Atomic Oil Co. v. Bardahl Oil
Co., 419 F.2d 1097, 1100-01 (10th Cir. 1969), cert. denied,
397 U.S. 1063 (1970), cited by Buddy Systems, can be read
as supporting the district court's theory, we disagree with
its holding.

III

Buddy Systems does not appear to embrace outright the
district court's theory that a bond is to be distinguished
from a security which is released. Rather, Buddy Systems'
argument is a variation on that theory; i.e., once a bond
has been executed and has established a basis for liability,
subsequent exoneration will not serve to oust all federal
courts of jurisdiction to determine liability.

Thus, under this second approach, the liability, once
established, is subsequently independent of the status of
the bond, even though there could have been no liability
without the initial execution of a bond. See Atomic Oil
Co., v. Bardahl Oil Co., supra, 419 F.2d at 1101; but see
Silvers v. TTC Industries, Inc., 484, F.2d 194, 199 (6th
Cir. 1973). The argument appears to be based upon the
avoidance of a paradox: adoption of a contrary result

would mean that federal jurisdiction could be abrogated unilaterally by an erroneous ruling of a single federal
court. This concern is completely unfounded, however.

Buddy Systems had the opportunity to raise the alleged
wrongful exoneration on its appeal from the permanent injunction. Exer-Genie, Inc. v. McDonald, supra. If Buddy
Systems had raised this issue and succeeded in having the
exoneration reversed as being premature and erroneous, it
could have moved the enjoining court for recovery on the
reinstated liability under Rule 65.1, Fed. R. Civ. P.,
Northeast Airlines, Inc. v. Nationwide Charters & Conventions, Inc., 413 F.2d 335, 338 (1st Cir. 1969),[9] or brought
an independent action to the reinstated liability in state
court or federal court under 28 U.S.C. §§1331 or 1352.
Thus our jurisdiction is not abrogated by the premature exoneration of the bond by the district court, but by Buddy
Systems' own failure to take advantage of the available
appellate remedies to have the alleged erroneous ruling
reversed.[10]

We are not unmindful of the underlying equities in
this case. Exer-Genie sought, and was the beneficiary of,

---

[9]After reversal of the issuance of the permanent injunction, but before initiating this section 1352 action,
Buddy Systems did move the issuing district court to reinstate the bond under Rule 65.1, but that court refused.
The propriety of that ruling is not before us.
[10]The exoneration was not implicitly reversed by the reversal of the permanent injunction on direct appeal. We
recognize that such a reversal provides a basis for
finding the preliminary injunction to have been wrongfully issued. Houghton v. Meyer, 208 U.S. 149, 159-60

the extraordinary equitable powers of a district court.
Having prevailed at trial, it then moved immediately for
an order exonerating its bond, thereby depriving Buddy
Systems of the protection the injunction bond is intended
to provide. Exer-Genie's haste in seeking the release of
its security, and its subsequent refusal to reinstate the
bond voluntarily or to acknowledge its liability under it,
do not enhance its position. But we should not make an
exception to what would otherwise be a simple and reason-
able rule in order to save jurisdiction for party blunders
if it will result in needless and unfortunate side effects.

We are here dealing with that exceptional case where
a party has been wrongfully enjoined, the district court
erroneously has exonerated the bond and the party, without
excuse, has failed to appeal this error. Rather than follow general principles of finality, Buddy Systems would
have us sanction a collateral attack on a routine district
court order by announcing a new jurisdictional rule for
our circuit. But at what cost? Although here Exer-Genie
secured its own bond by submitting a certificate of deposit,

_____

(1908). However, wrongful issuance is merely one element
of a cause of action on an injunction bond. Russell v.
Farley, supra, 105 U.S. at 441-46; Lawrence v. St. Louis-
S.F. Ry., 278 U.S. 228, 233, (1929); Page Communications
Eng'rs, Inc. v. Froehlke, 475 F.2d 994 (D.C. Cir. 1973).
The bond is still needed. There also must be damages
shown. If the enjoined party suffers no monetary damage,
he may not recover on a bond anyway and has no standing
to appeal an alleged wrongful exoneration. If there are
damages, it is incumbent upon the enjoined party to raise
the wrongful exoneration issue on appeal.

Buddy Systems' approach would be equally applicable to the case where the plaintiff has posted a surety bond. If we adopted its approach, sureties would be uncertain as to the termination of their liability and bonding costs could increase to reflect this uncertainty. Cf. Northern Trust Co. v. Edenborn, 39 F. Supp. 607 (W.D. La. 1941).[11] An increase in bonding costs would have a deterrent effect on the meritorious claims of indigents who seek provisional injunctive relief under Rule 65. See Dobbs, Provisional Injunctive Relief, supra, 52 N. Car. L. R. at 1112-17; Blood, Injunction Bonds: Equal Protection for the Indigent, 11 S. Tex. L.J. 16 (1969). District courts may well react to higher bond costs by exercising discretion to require bonds of lower amounts.[12] Thus, the net result of adopting a pro-recovery approach here could well be to subject more defendants to the prospect of inadequate relief for wrongfully issued injunctions.

In recognition of the problems likely to be generated by adopting the questionable jurisdictional exception advocated by Buddy Systems, we would want sound authority to chart the course. But Atomic Oil Co. v. Bardahl Oil Co., supra, does not provide us with an illumined path to follow. There is no discussion whatsoever in Atomic Oil of

---

[11] This may further burden the courts with lawsuits by sureties seeking a declaratory judgment as to their liability on an exonerated bond.
[12] Natural Resources Defense Council, Inc. v. Morton, 337 F. Supp. 167, 169 (D.D.C. 1971), motion for summary reversal denied, 458 F.2d 827 (D.C. Cir. 1972); cf. Friends of the Earth, Inc. v. Brinegar, 518 F.2d 322, 323 (9th Cir. 1975).

the court's source of jurisdiction. The defendant had
obtained recovery in an independent action on two injunction
bonds, one of which had been exonerated. The fact that
recovery was sought on both bonds, however, is not decisive
on the issue of section 1352 jurisdiction over the action
on the exonerated bond. Assuming the court had jurisdiction
over the claim on the existing bond pursuant to section
1352, it might have decided the claim on the exonerated
bond on a theory of pendent jurisdiction. See United Mine
Workers v. Gibbs, 383 U.S. 715 (1966). To the extent jurisdiction of the latter claim was based on section 1352,
we believe, as noted earlier, that Atomic Oil is wrong.

No other case can be cited in support of Buddy Systems'
position. Cases which have specifically entertained jurisdiction under section 1352 all involve suits of existing
security instruments. E.g., Hays Livestock Commission Co.
v. Maly Livestock Commission Co., 498 F.2d 925, 932 (10th
Cir. 1974); United States v. Western Casualty & Surety Co.,
429 F.2d 905, 906 (10th Cir. 1970); United States v. Kim-
rey, 489 F.2d 339, 341 (8th Cir. 1974).[13]

---

[13]Neither can Buddy Systems find support in reading treat-
ises. One treatise states only that a premature exoneration "will not immunize the principal or surety from what
otherwise might be the liability against them." 11 Wright
& Miller, supra, §2972, at 650. The authors cite two cases
for this proposition, both distinguishable from our case.
One is Atomic Oil; the other is Northeast Airlines, Inc. v.
Nationwide Chargers & Conventions, Inc. supra, where the
court reversed the exoneration on a direct appeal of the
original action for injunctive relief. In neither the cases
nor the context of the treatise authors' discussion was
there any reference to jurisdictional problems or section
1352.

Nor can it be persuasively argued that the refusal to find section 1352 jurisdiction over Exer-Genie's exonerated bond allows district judges unilaterally to abrogate federal jurisdiction. It must be conceded that this occurs every time a district judge decides an issue of jurisdiction incorrectly. Appellate courts exist to afford parties an opportunity to rectify these mistakes. Stoll v. Gottlieb, 305 U.S. 165, 171-75 (1938); see also Durfee v. Duke, 375 U.S. 106 (1963). Whether by neglect or strategy, Buddy Systems did not avail itself of a similar opportunity. We cannot save Buddy Systems from its blunder when the end result will be to override the clearly expressed intent of Congress in its allocation of federal jurisdiction.

REVERSED AND REMANDED.

UNITED STATES COURT OF APPEALS

FOR THE NINTH CIRCUIT

BUDDY SYSTEMS, INC.,
a California Corporation,   )
)
              Plaintiff-Appellee,   )   No. 74-1639
)
        -vs-   )
)
EXER-GENIE, INC., a Corporation,   )   ORDER
and E. E. HOLKESVICK,   )
)
              Defendants-Appellants.)
)

Before: ELY and WALLACE, Circuit Judges,
         and RENFREW,* District Judge

  Appellee's Petition for Rehearing is denied.

  The court refuses to consider the suggestion for
en banc rehearing by reason of the appellee's failure, in
making such suggestion, to comply with this court's Rule 12.

---

*Honorable Charles B. Renfrew, United States District Judge,
Northern District of California, sitting by designation.

32

RULE 65-c, Security

No restraining order or preliminary injunction shall issue except upon the giving of security by the applicant, in such sum as the court deems proper, for the payment of such costs and damages as may be incurred or suffered by any party who is found to have been wrongfully enjoined or restrained. No such security shall be required of the United States or of an officer or agency thereof.

The provisions of Rule 65.1 apply to a surety upon a bond or undertaking under this rule.

RULE 65.1 Security: Proceedings Against Sureties

Whenever these rules, including the Supplemental Rules for Certain Admiralty and Maritime Claims, require or permit the giving of security by a party, and security is given in the form of a bond or stipulation or other under- taking with one or more sureties, each surety submits himself to the jurisdiction of the court and irrevocably appoints the clerk of the court as his agent upon whom any papers affecting his liability on the bond or undertaking may be served. His liability may be enforced on motion and such notice of the motion as the court prescribes may be served on the clerk of the court, who shall forthwith mail copies to the sureties if their addresses are known.

28 U.S.C. § 1352

The district courts shall have original jurisdiction, concurrent with States courts, of any action on a bond executed under any law of the United States.

In The

SUPREME COURT OF THE UNITED STATES

Supreme Court, U. S.
F I L E D

APR 11 1977
4-11-77
MICHAEL RODAK, JR., CLERK

October Term, 1976
No. _____ 76-1056
—————— 76-1056

BUDDY SYSTEMS, INC., a corporation,

Petitioner,

vs.

EXER-GENIE, INC., a corporation, and
E. E. HOLKESVICK,

Respondents.

RESPONDENTS OPPOSITION TO
PETITION FOR WRIT OF CERTIORARI
FROM THE UNITED STATES COURT OF APPEALS
FOR THE NINTH CIRCUIT

CHARLES E. WILLS
700 South Flower Street, Suite 1120
Los Angeles, California 90017
(213) 688-7407

Attorney for Respondents

SUBJECT INDEX

1. Issue.

Does a district court have subject matter
jurisdiction under 28 U.S.C. 1352, for an action on
a bond . . . in the absence of any such bond at the
time of the filing of the action?

More specifically, is there such jurisdiction in a particular case where a Certificate of
Deposit was deposited with the Clerk pursuant to the
following provision in the Order Re Plaintiff's
Motion For Preliminary Injunction (Footnote 2, page
10 of Petition):

"Pursuant to Rule 65(C) of the
Federal Rules of Civil Procedure, the
plaintiffs herein shall give security
in the sum of One Hundred Thousand
Dollars ($100,000.00), by a corporate
surety bond, or by a treasury bond or a
certificate of deposit payable to Clerk,
United States District Court, for the
payment of such costs and damages as
may be incurred or suffered by any party
who is found to be wrongfully enjoined

or restrained".

which Certificate of Deposit was exonerated by
an order of the District Court prior to the filing
of the action purportedly based upon such bond?
(emphasis added)

2. Resume of Facts.

At the hearing on the preliminary injunction
in the patent infringement case, the petitioner
Buddy Systems, Inc. and the other defendants were
given the opportunity to continue to manufacture and
sell the accused exerciser, provided they posted
security for an award of damages in the event the
patent was held valid and infringed. Buddy Systems,
Inc. and the other defendants failed to post such
security.

Accordingly, the respondents Exer-Genie, Inc.
and E. E. Holkesvick posted a Certificate of Deposit
payable to Clerk, United States District Court, "for
the payment of such costs and damages as may be
incurred or suffered by any party who is found to be
wrongfully enjoined or restrained", and the

preliminary injunction was issued.

The petitioner Buddy Systems, Inc. failed to appeal the issuance of the preliminary injunction.

After a trial on the merits, the District Court held the patent to be valid and infringed, and Exer-Genie, Inc. and E. E. Holkesvick requested that the security be exonerated.

Before exonerating the security, the District Court gave Buddy Systems, Inc. a predetermined number of days within which to submit in writing, any authority which it might have as to why the security should not be exonerated. Buddy Systems, Inc. failed to submit any authority in support of its objection to the exoneration of the security.

In its Petition to this Court, Buddy Systems, Inc. erroneously states (page 3) that the district judge afforded Buddy Systems an opportunity to submit in writing any "argument" it might have in support of its objections, and Buddy Systems did submit such "argument" to the district judge in its Objections to the Findings of Fact and Conclusions

of Law and Judgment as proposed by Plaintiffs.
Buddy Systems, Inc. well knows the difference
between "arguments" and the "authorities"
requested by the Court, and it is unfortunate that
this Court should be subjected to such misstatement
of the facts.

On page 6 of the Petition, Buddy Systems,
Inc. states that the permanent injunction was lesser
in scope than the preliminary injunction. This is
incorrect. Both injunctions were of equal scope.
This should be obvious because the patent was held
valid and infringed, and the same accused
exerciser was involved in both the preliminary
injunction and the permanent injunction.

In its appeal of the Judgment and
Permanent Injunction in the patent infringement
case, Buddy Systems, Inc. failed to brief or argue
the exoneration of the security, and, accordingly,
the Court of Appeals did not reach that issue.

Thus, as pointed out by the Court of Appeals
in its Opinion which is the subject matter of this
Petition (page 19 of the Petition):

"On appeal, we reversed the district court's judgment and held that Exer-Genie's patents were invalid. Exer-Genie, Inc. v. McDonald, 453 F.2d 132 (9th Cir. 1971), cert. denied, 405, U.S. 1075, 1972). Buddy Systems did not challenge the exoneration of the bond as premature and erroneous   and we did not reach that issue on appeal." (emphasis added)

In short, by its failure to brief or argue the issue of the so-called premature and erroneous exoneration of the security, the petitioner Buddy Systems, Inc. waived any rights it might have had in that regard.

Buddy Systems, Inc. has "argued" that the release of the security by the Clerk on August 18, 1969, was not noted on the Docket Sheet, and Buddy Systems, Inc. did not discover that the security was actually released until after the decision of the Court of Appeals on September 14, 1971.

There is no evidence to support this "argument" and it flies in the face of the Judgment of the District Court which was filed and entered on August 15, 1969, and which provided in paragraph 4 thereof that:

"The Clerk shall return to the Plaintiffs, the security which they gave for the issuance of the preliminary injunction". [C. 142]

It would be obvious to the most inexperienced, that if a party went to the trouble and expense of seeking an order to obtain the release of $100,000.00, and such an Order was signed and filed, the party would promptly reobtain possession of the $100,000.00.

3. There is no direct conflict among the Circuits regarding the right to bring an action upon a bond . . . in the absence of a bond.

The overwhelming weight of authority is that in the absence of a bond or other posted security, no damages can be awarded for the wrongful issuance of a preliminary injunction.

The petitioner Buddy Systems, Inc. argues that a conflict exists among the Circuits regarding the right to bring an action on a bond . . . in the absence of a bond, relying primarily upon Atomic Oil Co. v. Bardahl Oil Co., 419 F.2d 1097 (10 Cir. 1969), cert. denied, 397 U.S. 1063 (1970).

The petitioner also states (page 5 of Petition) that the Circuit Court below summarily stated that it disagreed with the holding of Atomic Oil Co., and that the facts in the present case are similar to those in Atomic Oil Co.

Not So. The facts were different and the basis of the holding in Atomic Oil Co. is not clear.

With regard to the holding of <u>Atomic Oil</u>
<u>Co.</u>, the Circuit Court below stated:

"in recognition of the problems
likely to be generated by adopting the
questionable jurisdictional exception
advocated by Buddy Systems, we would
want sound authority to chart the course.
But <u>Atomic Oil Co. v. Bardahl Oil Co.</u>,
<u>supra</u>, does not provide us with an
illumined path to follow. There is no
discussion whatsoever in <u>Atomic Oil</u> of
the court's source of jurisdiction. The
defendant had obtained recovery in an
independent action on two injunction
bonds, one of which had been exonerated.
The fact that recovery was sought on
both bonds, however, is not decisive on
the issue of section 1352 jurisdiction
over the action on the exonerated bond.
Assuming the court had jurisdiction over
the claim on the existing bond pursuant to
Section 1352, it might have decided the

the claim on the exonerated bond on
a theory of pendent jurisdiction. See
United Mine Workers v. Gibbs, 383 U.S.
715 (1966). To the extent jurisdiction
of the latter claim was based on section
1352, we believe, as noted earlier, that
Atomic Oil is wrong.

No other case can be cited in
support of Buddy Systems' position."

4. If it were determined that
district courts have subject matter
jurisdiction under 28 U.S.C. 1352
for an action on a bond . . . where
there is no such bond . . . the
results would be chaotic.

As pointed out by the Circuit Court
(pp. 27-28 of the Petition), if the theory
advanced by Buddy Systems, Inc. were to be adopted,
sureties would be uncertain as to the termination
of their liability and bonding costs could increase
to reflect this uncertainty, and such an increase

in bonding costs would have a deterent effect on the meritorious claims of indigents who seek provisional injunctive relief under Rule 65.

And, if district courts were to react to higher bond costs by requiring bonds of lower amounts, the net result could well be to subject more defendants to the prospect of inadequate relief for wrongfully issued injunctions.

5. Conclusion.

The petitioner Buddy Systems, Inc. is in its present position because:

(a) it failed to appeal the issuance of the preliminary injunction in the patent infringement action,

(b) it failed to submit authorities to the District Court as to why the security should not be exonerated pending appeal, which the District Court specifically requested it to do prior to exonerating the security, and

(c) it failed to brief and argue the issue of the exoneration of the security on the appeal of the patent infringement action.

Thus, as stated by the Circuit Court (p. 30 of Petition):

"Nor can it be persuasively argued that the refusal to find section 1352 jurisdiction over Exer-Genie's exonerated bond allows district judges unilaterally to abrogate federal jurisdiction. It must be conceded that this occurs every time a district judge decides an issue of jurisdiction incorrectly. Appellate courts exist to afford parties an opportunity to rectify these mistakes. Stoll v. Gottlieb, 305 U.S. 165, 171-75 (1938); See also Durfee v. Duke, 375, 375 U.S. 106 (1963). Whether by neglect or strategy, Buddy Systems did not avail itself of a similar opportunity. We cannot save Buddy Systems from its blunder when the end result will be to override the clearly expressed intent of Congress in its allocation of federal jurisdiction."

WHEREFORE, this Court is respectfully urged to deny the Petition of Buddy Systems, Inc.

Respectfully submitted,

Charles E. Wills

Los Angeles, California

April 6 , 1977.